NIN

A PROSE POEM
IN THE MANNER OF
MATSUO BASHO

Inscribed to my brother David
Older and Wiser

BY

MIKE BANNISTER

ORPHEAN PRESS

2019

'The journey itself is my home'
Matsuo Basho

First published in 2019 by Orphean Press
10 Heath Close, Polstead Heath, Colchester CO6 5BE

Typeset in eleven- on thirteen-point ITC Golden Cockerel,
printed and bound in Great Britain by Peter Newble:
10 Heath Close, Polstead Heath, Colchester CO6 5BE
peter@newble.com ❖ *http://www.newble.com/*

ISBN 978-1-908198-19-8

British Library Cataloguing in Publication Data
A catalogue record for this book is
available from the British Library.

THE WAY NORTH

NEAR midnight on the path to Wales; a village, a factory gate, a regiment behind me, and little traffic on the road. The *Wrekin*, my mute companion for too long now, is a pitch-black whale to the south. I wait in a pool of lamp-light, almost an hour until a low black French saloon draws up. Do I know the way to *Anglesey*? Can I show him? Our fortunes change. He will find his ferry port, and I should be among mountains before sunrise. We set out together, traveller and guide . . .

He hails from *Rouen*, an architect with designs on Dublin. The old trunk road winds and rises, bridges the *Severn*, skirts the sinuous *Dee*. A glowing dial accrues the kilometres. We achieve *Berwyn Heights*, and span *Ruthin* moor, swing through forest and fen. In less than two hours we come to the *Capel* junction, where our ways diverge. I direct my deliverer onwards, north by west. We exchange handshakes, thanks and good wishes. I climb out, and find myself alone with my rucksack in the night . . .

To the west, a moonlit vista, a silver lake, a winding skein of trout pools, and far beyond, a riotous mountain ring, black against stars; *Eryri*, mountains of longing. It has been almost two years. I breathe deep, inhale the sweet cool air. Only the far-off noise of water proves this is no dream. I wriggle into my pack-straps; twelve miles left to stride before I find the stone house beside the cataract, and good friends waiting . . .

Striding out alone
in step with the universe
affiliated.

The freedoms of youth
endless days and starlit nights
singular moments.

Iron gates swing wide
hearing the dry leaves whisper
spiral thoughts vanish.

Holyhead Road (A5)

IDYLL

HE stirs, bright sunbeams prick his sleep encrusted eyes. The four who love him most stand over him. Silence, except for the murmur of insects. Tenderly he is lifted from his jewelled nest. Indoors they tuck him down to finish out his dream. His pink chin pollen dusted, and with a hint of new cider . . .

Lunch in that peaceful place was a long communion, asparagus maybe, through to cheese and strawberries. Always the talk would wind on, of the war and cities burned, lost brothers, sons and daughters, contingencies, coping, making do, mending, healing, and the aching want of an end to it all . . .

Unobserved that day, he fades from view. The inner parlour door, unlatched, invites; scrubbed table, pine chair, tumbler, cloth-covered jug of thick sweet apple-fire. He climbs up, pours a demi-draught, sips slowly as he has seen old men sip . . .

Warm afternoon in the Cotswold; he wanders out to find a cleft in the rock garden, stone the colour of saxon gold. He settles among cushions of saxifrage and lavender; the bees accommodate him. Nestled there, wondering about apples, a clearwater brook, a staring cow, sleep floats him into forgetfulness . . .

How we are wakened	A time out of war
time we are given to dream	summer orchards, brook and stream
schools before schooling.	engines in darkness.

Untempered so, we
grow, imagine, more or less
ten thousand things.

Willersey, Gloucestershire

AT WISTMAN'S WOOD

P ETER Tavy, Dartmoor, east by north from Stephen's Grave along *Lych Way*—The Coffin Road—a standing stone marks *White Barrow*. Here the land falls away, south. We ford *Prison Leat*, and make camp under *Blackbrook Head*. A chill night, with showers then starry skies . . .

First light: in a place of stones, granite Tors, huge unfinished stone loaves, weird rows and circles; a wild place, where the sun comes late. The sweet air is electric with a thousand histories. We climb steep-walled *Lydford Tor*, and so to *Beardown*, following the carved crosses. By *West River* stands *Wistman's Wood*, its granite spine clothed in a squat forest of hobgoblin oaks hung, bole and branch, with fibrous lichen, pale-grey and brittle dry . . .

We pitch tents on scattered levels of rich grass. There is an island boulder in the stream where we propose a fire. I crawl into the shade, searching for underwood. The oaks are low, serpentine, tricky to negotiate. I take to the boulders and soon feel drawn to scale the upper ridge. The rock is dry, pleasant to move on. Minutes later, with both hands on the final slab, I peer over . . .

What meets my eye astonishes. Below, no more than ten feet off, is Lord Peregrine himself, stripping red meat from the breast of a moorland bird. He looks up; transfixes me with an imperious glare. I hold his gaze no more than seconds, then dip down, lowering myself away, breathing slow . . .

Clear of the trees again, we make our fire, lichen, fine twigs, dry sticks then thicker stuff. The flare of it warms me, a red-gold cavern in the falling dark. I ruminate on my brief audience with the spirit of the place, his fierce, peat-dark, poker-player's eye, the awful power of it, whose dread authority, for a fleeting moment, I usurped . . .

When least imagined
the mysteries of nature
become visible.

Where the trees endure
history itself endures
memory's green thread.

A death among trees
scent of the struggle to live
fresh blood and wood-smoke.

Devonshire

3

SILVER SPOON

CHRISTMAS Eve, stars and a frost, a walk across fields, a coach ride out of town, the loud 'ching' of a brass lever clock, the night-shift proceeds. The pound-a-day teacher transmogrified, booted and wrapped against the cold, becomes a monitor . . .

Your dominion? A lamp-lit factory yard, flagged, thick with the cloying sweetness of wet clay. A gurgling pit of hot beet-wash batters an iron grille; you make an off-tilt round of rank necessities. Overhead, a towering concrete stack, visible for miles, unfurls its weird acrylic smear against the dark . . .

Your tools: an iron barrow and a long steel-handled claw; the task until sunrise, to keep the gully flowing free and clear, through Christmas nights: Time, Time and a half, Double-time, Triple-time even, if the feast falls on Sunday . . .

On the hour, you haul a hundred-weight of slaked lime, tumble its choking dust into the pit, and, coughing, stow the folded bag inside. Between times, you stamp your boots, and wheel out the hot rakings to a rancid mountain . . .

Wet nights, you slip into the engine shed, climb aboard the roaring box, warm your bones, peruse a line or two of Sophocles, before bending again to the mindless-ness of passing time . . .

First light: you sip from a flask, feeling no urge to eat. At six, the siren sounds redemption. You prop the barrow, hang the claw, and slope wearily to join the others for the ride back. Christmas Day; on the bus you drift in and out of sleep, and dream the sound of morning bells.

Hard labour, late work
birthright of the dispossessed
a sweetness distilled.

Beyond certainty
streams of consequence flow from
our least adventures.

Lion in hot sand
wild bees in a hollow skin
honey from the sting.

Allscott, Shropshire

TIDE WAY

LATE Autumn, wind north east, force five, soon to veer, soon to rise. We slip anchor in *Slaughden Pool*, find mid-river, seven fathoms; long keel slicing the ebb-tide ...

Low cloud, like knotted steel, no boat on the river but *Rionnag*, no birds flying. We steer between whale-backs of slick mud, counting wands, south by west, downriver: *Horse Pool, Home Reach, Blackstakes*. Three mile out, *Alde* becomes *Ore*, winds through galaxies of anchored boats by *Orford Town*, the quay deserted ...

Havergate Isle north-end, a gybe into *Gull Channel* eight, ten, twelve fathoms. *Butley Creek* opens. Stealthy Vikings in our own pine double-ender, we nudge close to the ruined dock. Sheltered so, we feast on good bread and salami, warm our hands. Low-water springs, here oyster-catchers, curlews and plovers also feed ...

By *Lower Gull*, tide turns, wind rises. At *Dove Buoy* we trim our tan sails, bucking north along *The Narrows*. Far side of *Orford Beach*, you sense the roar of big surf. Flood-tide, seethes now, adds five knots more on the surge. In a hiss of white water the stem cleaves, foam furling ...

Wide canvas, fat with the gale, shroud wires whistle and thrum, sheets hard-hauled to perfect inclinations. She creaks, tightening, heels a little, tunes herself; this lithe aeolian thing, oak, pine, rope and canvas, sings of the sea, and glides ...

At heaven's hand now: there's a wild joy in free speed, flight almost. We ride, for a while the bare force of nature: power of the sun, power of the moon. Landmarks reel by; church, village, moorings, ferry, lighthouse, there, here, and gone again, as her straight wake fades astern ...

Weary at last, in spitting rain. we round up to the anchorage: placid shallows by the mussel beds, where long-legged waders lean and probe. We coil down, pump her dry, make all secure, and prepare to row ashore ...

Who traces unseen
paths of wind and water
travels with the gods.

At one with tides
the universal moon-force
sublime residence.

Orange-pip hull form
thumb and finger, wind and wave,
the go of sailing.

Suffolk

5

CONSCRIPT

FIRST light finds him on the northbound platform of a border town. Assistant gunner, death reckoner, target-plotter, able to assess terrain, distance and elevation, make allowances for wind-strength and humidity, manipulate the barrage, enabling all hell in steel, fire and cordite. Daily he thanks his gods there is no current war ...

He sports an ill-cut battle dress in serge the colour of dung, prickly, chafing at cuff and collar, cinched with ungainly belt, gaiters and pack-straps all chalked in a paler green, boots black and glistening. He lumbers a canvas kit-sack; black-stencilled G.R.A ... 287, his sole identity for two years to come. Save for a travel warrant, his pockets all are void ...

A train pulls in, steam driven. It coughs, barks and hisses under him, curled in a corner seat, all day and most of the night; crossing the coal field, the salt plain, furnaced steel towns, vistas of grit-stone and white rock, moorland mile on mile ...

At York, a stranger wakes him, proposes tea in return for a peculiar favour: to keep guard over his, the stranger's, wife, who does not appear, and will not. In a neat leather 'Gladstone' his love, cremated, lies beside him, bound for America pending permission from the consulate. A deal is struck that somehow lifts his spirit ...

Twilight comes and goes, night vigils at unknown crossing places, until he reports to the Redesdale Barrack. A wall-eyed sergeant dispatches him to a foul canteen, then to a tent; warns him not to settle in. 'Tomorrow you leave for the east, and some other camp along the coast.' ...

Permitting others to direct which road we take denies our compass.	The heart prevented, kindness hides under sharp stones smoke and noise of war.

War's friend? Disunion.
And the enemy of war?
Love universal.

Oswestry—Barnard Castle

THOR'S CAVE

A T *Flash* by *Brand Side*, the *Manifold* is a slow trickle in field-grass; a cock-stride from *Dove Springs* with more than twenty mile between. We are four students, out to trace the twin rivers, breezing downhill, singing somewhat, through white crags and rain soaked forest ...

The force meanders, clear, deep and louder with each fall. At the confluence, a fisherman's inn. Too bedraggled for the parlour, we settle for a pine table and a log-fire in the rear canteen. Ale flows, plain food passes round, we steam in the glow of it, learning what friendship is ...

Upstream now, we track the *Dove* herself. She winds toward us, vanishes sometimes, underground, chuckling in the dark. Then sheer above, we sense the vast cavern's eye, and scramble up into its shade, its silence, our shelter for the night; a dry place, with the un-earthly tang of age, pale calcites, alabasterine, things un-nameable ...

We find our ledges, drape out the wet gear, spread sleeping rolls and rest, while a late shower rattles on the trees two hundred feet below. Is it earth's whisper, applause perhaps? or else some echo of beings past, hunters, herdsmen, fugitives—others here before ...

The day fades, blueish, crepuscular at first, as all the roof bats, ten thousand surely, black flittering silhouettes, go pillaging among the moth shoals. Before I've counted half the stars, sleep intervenes ...

And then the morning: measured by the slow drip of last night's rain, seeping through sod and crevice. It taps my shoulder, at times irregular, insists I come to life ...

Rain on its wild ride
sky to sea, ushers me near
to the soul of her.

Falling asleep there,
wrapped in the earth's rough blanket
past and future meet.

Sunrise, we gaze out
hatchlings ready to depart
the shell of the earth.

Dove Dale

7

TRAVERSE

JULY, high summer, the green bus puts us down by *Ogwen Falls*. We take a sheep track, head south into the mile-wide cirque, a blue-green amphitheatre, silent vertiginous, reflected in a glassy pool ...

The mountain air is sweet and clear, our sense of liberation joyous without end; a new world, ours for the day, not a soul to be seen. We tramp steadily, alpine style intending not to rest. Dvořák's ninth rings in head and heart: *Largo*. After a half-hour we gain the lake shore; a still mirror, across which no bird will ever fly, or so the legend tells ...

We hop boulders to cross a noisy cataract, and pause awhile under the the sheer north-west face. Climbing it will take three hours or so: a blunt rib, of rough dry rhyolite, easy scrambling, then steeper work. We pair off on two separate ropes, inching our way via basalt slabs grooves and corners, rising slowly south-east for the most part, then by a ridge, south-west ...

We balance, toes and fingers, make incremental steps, conserving energy, roping through, changing leads; the elemental joy of climbing, close as close to mother earth and not so very far from oblivion. A single mis-step might be the end of it ...

Sunset finds us at the top. Half a mile west, we wait at the col. An hour goes by and darkness falls before the others come down, exhilarated. We descend, south-side—sometimes *au derrière*—steep heather, bracken, boulder and bush. The path by night is ill-defined. Seven hundred feet below, village lights flicker. We find the wall, follow it to a gate, a yard, then a byre, where geese and a barking dog announce our coming home ...

Zen of wild mountains
stone, water, wind, sun and sky,
complete awareness.

Ant on the high wall
what is vertigo to him.
or fear of falling?

In memoriam
John Rice, Phil Kemp, Walt Meredith
who rest in far fields.

Nant Francon—Nant Peris, Gwynedd

8

STRANGE MEETINGS

A WATER-snake. Two motes of diamond dust shimmying down river, just clear of the meniscus, then a langourous whiplash, near a metre of it, winding cosine curves; a live thrusting thing, strangely fearful, whose grip on existence seems somehow finer than mine. Is it envy stirs me? or some deeper primal loathing...

Sensing ambush between boat and alder pilings, he seems to panic, writhes in a frantic wash-dance, bright olive braid, water beaded; his burred belly-scales working the soft moss; he levitates to post his gold-flecked serpent head between the boards, and with two less-hurried heaves, escapes, deep into the wet clay caverns of the rhond...

Past the place now, still prickling, I hold the thought of that chance meeting; the miles of labyrinthine dumb green sedge and sediment, a quiet kingdom of things other, unknown, un-nameable, enduring, and he the bright green master of it all...

Back Road Echoes; of a hot summer in Roussillon, another lordly rock snake, sentinel of the cataract; a swallow flies clean through the granite hill; a painted chapel wall, blue on ochre, with five mounted knights, their cruel lances goading Him to Calvary...

In *Roussillon*, M. Agricole tends vines, feeds escargot fat on sorrel leaves, while Madame Agricole—*dea nutrix*—attentive to the stranger's new-made sonnet, draws him close to her, bestows a kiss upon his ruffled crown, then fills his glass with dark red Corbières...

First recognitions
of memory and desire
are never purchased.

Meetings with strangers
their meanings and metaphors
times bright legacies.

Divine convergence
Mother Earth herself, at home
in fair Roussillon!

St Olaves, Norfolk, 2005 & Roussilon

ACKNOWLEDGEMENTS

THE author wishes to thank Ann Bannister for her critical advice on the manuscript, and Amber H. Pletts for her cover illustration in pen and ink. Members of the Portfolio Group at Suffolk Poetry Society have offered useful comments on some of the nine poems here.

MATSUO BASHO

MATSUO Basho (1644–1694) was the most highly respected poet of the Edo period in Japan. He was recognised for his works in the collaborative *haiku non renga* form. His work was prolific and is now acknowledged internationally as a major part of Japan's great literary heritage. In later life Basho made several journeys throughout Japan, and produced fascinating journals, including *The Narrow Road to the Deep North, Back Roads to Far Towns* and *Travel Sketches*. These later works consist of poetic prose passages, interspersed with *haiku*, which seem to encapsulate the emotional and philosophical essence of his journeys.

MIKE BANNISTER

MIKE Bannister was born Alvechurch, Worcestershire. Following military service, he worked in community schools, mostly in inner-cities. He lives now in Suffolk with his wife, Ann. Mike chairs Swan Poets, a venue for working poets in his home-town of Halesworth.

His previous publications are *Greenstreet Fragments* (Orphean Press, 2003), *Pocahontas in Ludgate* (Arrowhead Press, 2007), *Orinsay Poems* (Orphean Press, 2012), *The Green Man* (Bibliotecha Universalis, 2014) *Late Poems, 2007–2016* (Orphean Press, 2017). His poetry has appeared in magazines regionally and nationally, earning a variety of awards and commendations.